Learn to Draw
AMAZING ANIMALS

www.av2books.com

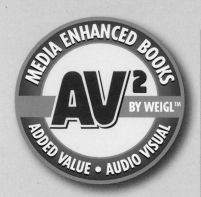

MEDIA ENHANCED BOOKS
AV²
BY WEIGL™
ADDED VALUE • AUDIO VISUAL

AV² provides enriched content that supplements and complements this book. Weigl's AV² books strive to create inspired learning and engage young minds in a total learning experience.

Your AV² Media Enhanced books come alive with...

Audio
Listen to sections of the book read aloud.

Key Words
Study vocabulary, and complete a matching word activity.

Go to **www.av2books.com**, and enter this book's unique code.

Video
Watch informative video clips.

Quizzes
Test your knowledge.

BOOK CODE

P326175

Embedded Weblinks
Gain additional information for research.

Slide Show
View images and captions, and prepare a presentation.

AV² by Weigl brings you media enhanced books that support active learning.

Try This!
Complete activities and hands-on experiments.

... and much, much more!

Published by AV² by Weigl
350 5th Avenue, 59th Floor
New York, NY 10118
Website: www.weigl.com   www.av2books.com

Library of Congress Cataloging-in-Publication Data

Amazing animals / edited by Jordan McGill.
     p. cm. -- (Learn to draw)
 Includes index.
 ISBN 978-1-61690-856-0 (hardcover : alk. paper) -- ISBN 978-1-61690-862-1 (pbk. : alk. paper) -- ISBN 978-1-61690-985-7 (online)
 1. Animals in art--Juvenile literature. 2. Drawing--Technique--Juvenile literature. I. McGill, Jordan.
 NC780.A46 2011
 743.6--dc23

                         2011020309

Printed in the United States of America in North Mankato, Minnesota
1 2 3 4 5 6 7 8 9 0 15 14 13 12 11

062011
WEP290411

Project Coordinator: Jordan McGill
Art Director: Terry Paulhus

Every reasonable effort has been made to trace ownership and to obtain permission to reprint copyright material. The publishers would be pleased to have any errors or omissions brought to their attention so that they may be corrected in subsequent printings.

Weigl acknowledges Getty Images as its primary image supplier for this title.

Contents

2 . . . . AV² Book Code

4 . . . . Why Draw?

5 . . . . Amazing Animals

6 . . . . Meet the Alligator

10 . . . . Meet the Dolphin

14 . . . . Meet the Elephant

18 . . . . Meet the Gorilla

22 . . . . Meet the Lion

26 . . . . Meet the Shark

30 . . . . Test Your Knowledge of Amazing Animals

31 . . . . Draw an Environment/ Glossary

32 . . . . Log on to av2books.com

6

10

14

18

22

26

Why Draw?

Drawing is easier than you think. Look around you. The world is made of shapes and lines. By combining simple shapes and lines, anything can be drawn. An orange is just a circle with a few details added. A flower can be a circle with ovals drawn around it. An ice cream cone can be a triangle topped with a circle. Most anything, no matter how complicated, can be broken down into simple shapes.

circle

oval

circle →

circle

triangle →

Drawing helps people make sense of the world. It is a way to reduce an object to its simplest form, say our most personal feelings and thoughts, or show others objects from our **imagination**. Drawing an object can help you learn how it fits together and works.

What shapes do you see in this car?

It is fun to put the world onto a page, but it is also a good way to learn. Learning to draw even simple objects introduces the skills needed to fully express oneself visually. Drawing is an excellent form of **communication** and improves people's imagination.

Practice drawing your favorite animals in this book to learn the basic skills necessary to draw. You can use those skills to create your own drawings.

Amazing Animals

Drawing the animals in this book is a great way to learn about the different parts and features that make these animals successful in their environment. As you draw each part of the animals in this book, consider how that part benefits the animal. Think about how the animal would survive without that feature.

Incredible animals that defy belief live in all parts of the world. These animals find everything they need to live in their environment. In nature, they live best without interference from humans. They have adapted to be very successful in their environments. Some animals, such as the shark, have lived successfully for millions of years.

Meet the Alligator

Alligators belong to a group of animals called reptiles. Reptiles have hard, scaly skin all over their bodies. Snakes, lizards, and turtles are also reptiles.

Alligators spend part of their time on land and part of their time in rivers or lakes. They are expert swimmers. Alligators stay near the surface of the water so that they can breathe air.

Eyes
Alligators have good eyesight and can see well underwater. They have a clear eyelid that covers their eyes underwater. This allows them to see underwater without irritation.

Nostrils
Nostrils on top of the alligator's head let the animal breathe while it hides underwater.

Jaws
Alligators have very sharp teeth for catching and eating **prey**. Alligators eat only meat.

Plates
Tough, scaly skin protects the alligator from other animals.

Tail
An alligator pushes itself through the water with its strong tail. Sometimes, an alligator will use its tail to knock other animals down.

Claws
Alligators have five claws on each front foot and four claws on each back foot. They have webbing between their claws. This helps them swim.

How to Draw an
Alligator

1 Start with a simple stick figure of the alligator. Use circles for the head and body, ovals for the feet, and lines for the limbs and tail.

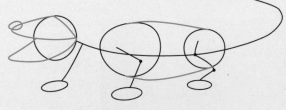

2 Now, join the two body circles together with a smooth, curved line. Also, draw the jaws and a small circle on the tip of the upper jaw. This will become the alligator's **snout**.

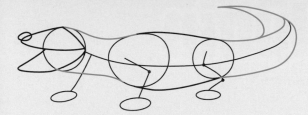

3 Next, join the circles for the head and body with curved lines, and draw the tail around the tail line.

4 In this step, draw the legs and tongue, as shown.

5 Next, draw the webbed paws and a lump on the head, which is the eye on the other side.

6 Draw the other eye and teeth. Also, draw scales on the body and tail using small curved lines.

7 Draw lumps on the back and tail, and add checkered lines on the belly for scales.

8 Erase the extra lines and the stick figure frame.

9 Color the picture.

Meet the Dolphin

Dolphins are friendly and smart animals that always seem to be smiling. They live in natural bodies of water around the world.

Many people confuse dolphins with fish. Dolphins are **marine mammals**. They breathe air just like humans. Every few minutes, a dolphin rises to the surface of the ocean to breathe through a blowhole on top of their head.

Blowhole

The blowhole is used for breathing. Dolphins keep the blowhole shut when underwater. They only open it to breathe.

Melon

The melon, located on the forehead, helps send underwater sounds.

Beak

Inside a dolphin's beak are teeth. A dolphin's teeth are cone-shaped with sharp points. They are used to grab and hold on to food.

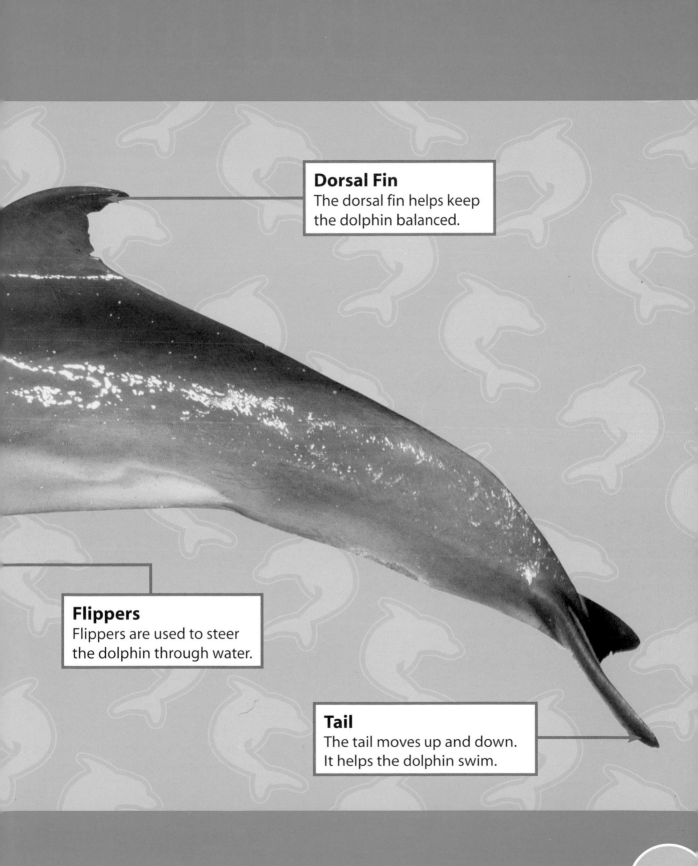

Dorsal Fin
The dorsal fin helps keep the dolphin balanced.

Flippers
Flippers are used to steer the dolphin through water.

Tail
The tail moves up and down. It helps the dolphin swim.

How to Draw a Dolphin

1 Start with a simple stick figure of the dolphin. Use circles for the body, ovals for the snout and head, and lines for the fins.

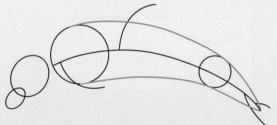

2 Now, join the two body circles together with a smooth, curved line, in the shape of a curved teardrop.

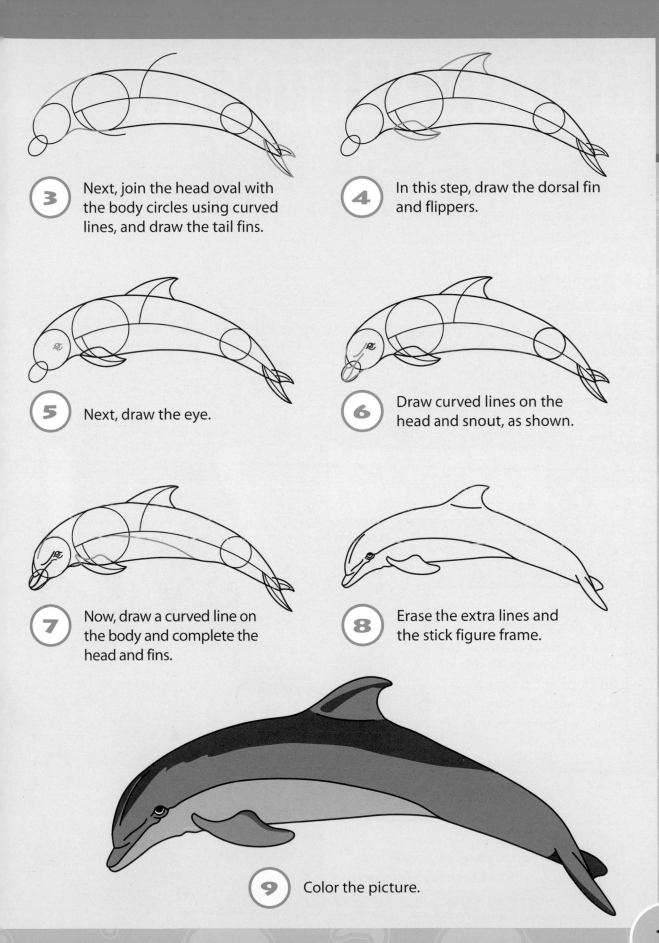

3 Next, join the head oval with the body circles using curved lines, and draw the tail fins.

4 In this step, draw the dorsal fin and flippers.

5 Next, draw the eye.

6 Draw curved lines on the head and snout, as shown.

7 Now, draw a curved line on the body and complete the head and fins.

8 Erase the extra lines and the stick figure frame.

9 Color the picture.

Meet the Elephant

The elephant is the largest animal that lives on land. It has a huge, bulky body and a long nose called a trunk. Two curved tusks grow on either side of the trunk. Tusks are long, sharp teeth. They are made of a hard material called ivory.

Tusks
Sharp tusks are useful for digging up plants to eat.

Trunk
A trunk can make a loud noise like a trumpet to call other elephants. To drink, an elephant sucks up water with its trunk. Then, it sprays the water into its mouth.

Legs
Strong legs with wide feet support the elephant's body.

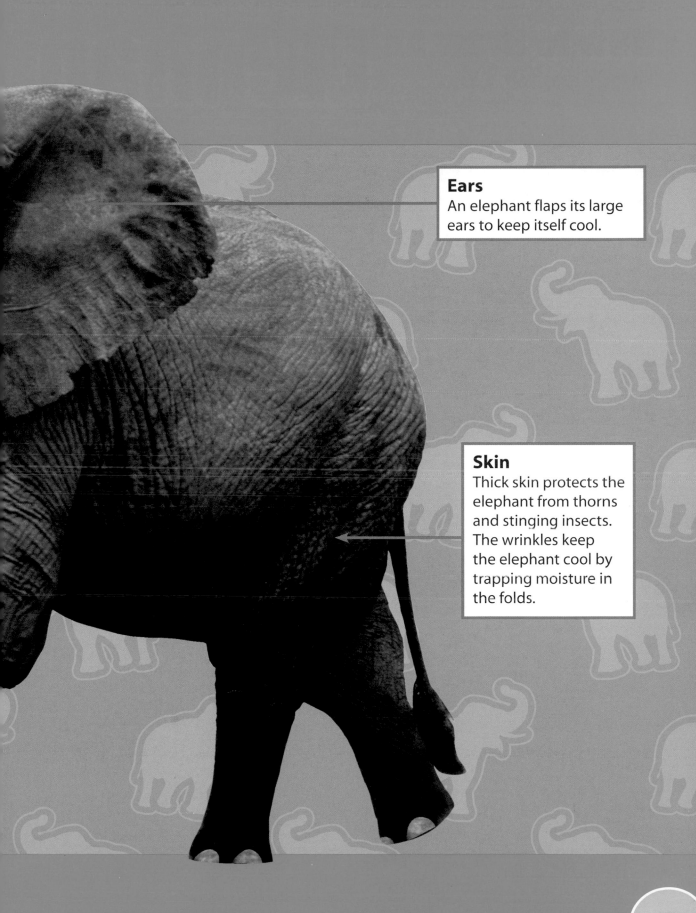

Ears
An elephant flaps its large ears to keep itself cool.

Skin
Thick skin protects the elephant from thorns and stinging insects. The wrinkles keep the elephant cool by trapping moisture in the folds.

How to Draw an Elephant

1 Start with a simple stick figure of the elephant. Use a circle for the body, ovals for the head and trunk, and lines for the limbs.

2 Now, join the head oval and body circle with a smooth, curved line. Also, draw the trunk with curved lines, as shown.

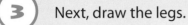

3 Next, draw the legs.

4 In this step, draw the eyes and tail.

5 Next, draw the ears.

6 Now, draw the tusks and nails.

7 Draw curved lines on the head, body, and ears for the wrinkles. Also, draw hair on the tail.

8 Erase the extra lines and the stick figure frame.

9 Color the picture.

Meet the Gorilla

Gorillas are big, strong, intelligent animals. They live in the forests of West and Central Africa.

Most people think that gorillas are scary animals. Gorillas are very calm, peaceful, and kind. These big, fearsome-looking animals are **herbivores**.

Gorillas are the largest members of the great ape family.

Face
Gorillas have no hair on their face. Each gorilla has its own unique facial features.

Nose
Gorillas have distinct noses. Researchers can tell one gorilla from another by the shape of its nose.

Hands
Gorilla hands have five fingers and an **opposable** thumb. Gorillas use their hands to eat. They mostly eat plants.

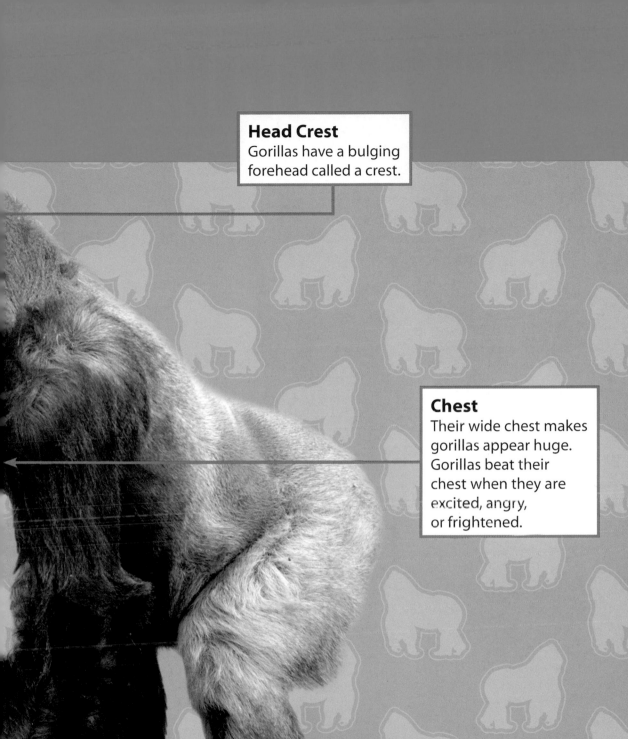

Head Crest
Gorillas have a bulging forehead called a crest.

Chest
Their wide chest makes gorillas appear huge. Gorillas beat their chest when they are excited, angry, or frightened.

Feet
Gorilla feet have five toes and an opposable toe.

How to Draw a Gorilla

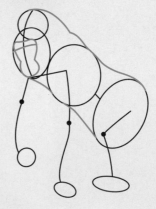

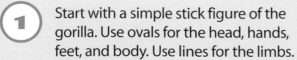

1 Start with a simple stick figure of the gorilla. Use ovals for the head, hands, feet, and body. Use lines for the limbs.

2 Now, join the head and body ovals together with curved lines. Also, draw curved lines on the face, as shown.

3 Next, draw the arms and legs.

4 In this step, draw the hands and feet.

5 Next, draw the nose, mouth, ear, and nails.

6 Now, draw the eyes.

7 Draw hair on the head, body, and limbs.

8 Erase the extra lines and the stick figure frame.

9 Color the picture.

Meet the Lion

A lion is a large animal with four strong legs and sharp teeth. A female lion is called a lioness. Lions are **mammals**, which are animals that feed their babies milk and have hair or fur on their bodies.

Lions belong to the same family as pet cats, but a person could not keep a mighty lion as a pet. It is one of the fiercest **predators** on Earth.

Eyes
A lion's large eyes help it to see well at night.

Back Claws
Lions' back paws have four sharp claws. A lion's claws can be three inches (7.6 cm) long.

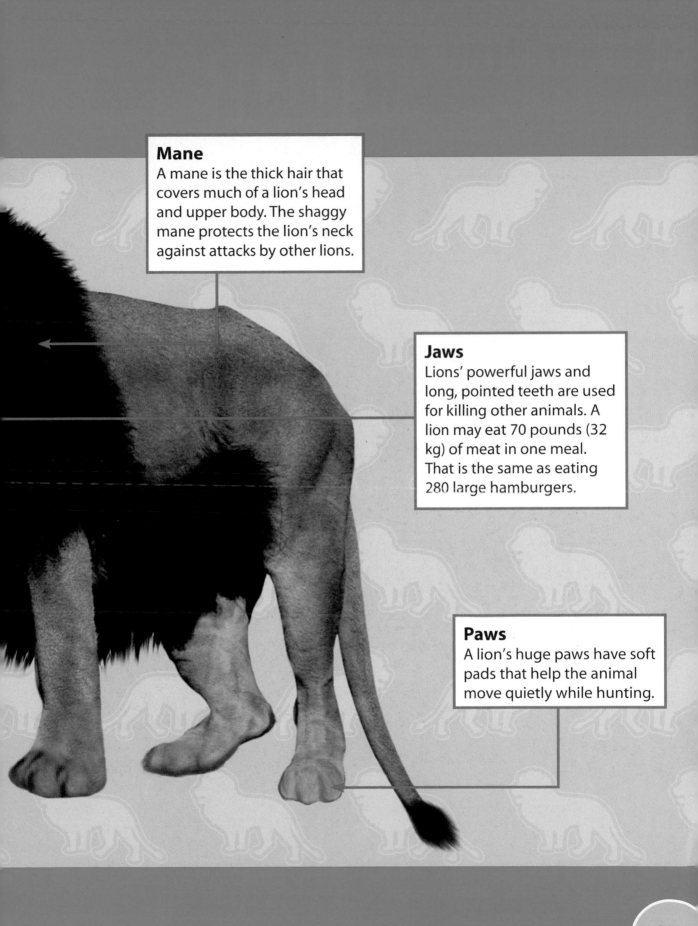

Mane
A mane is the thick hair that covers much of a lion's head and upper body. The shaggy mane protects the lion's neck against attacks by other lions.

Jaws
Lions' powerful jaws and long, pointed teeth are used for killing other animals. A lion may eat 70 pounds (32 kg) of meat in one meal. That is the same as eating 280 large hamburgers.

Paws
A lion's huge paws have soft pads that help the animal move quietly while hunting.

How to Draw a Lion

1 Start with a simple stick figure of the lion. Use circles for the head and body, ovals for the snout and feet, and lines for the limbs and tail.

2 Now, join the two body circles together with a smooth, curved line. Also, draw a large circle around the head. This will become the lion's mane.

3 Next, draw the ears and mouth.

4 In this step, draw the legs, as shown.

5 Next, draw the tail and paws.

6 Now, draw the eyes, nose, whiskers, and nails.

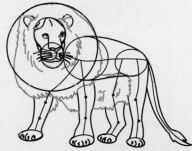

7 Draw the mane and hair around the head, body, and tail.

8 Erase the extra lines and the stick figure frame.

9 Color the picture.

Meet the Shark

Snout
A shark's snout is used to smell, but not to breathe. The great white shark can smell one drop of blood in 25 gallons (95 liters) of water.

Great white sharks are large, meat-eating fish. They are the most dangerous of all sharks.

The great white shark's skin is covered with a layer of tiny teeth called denticles. These denticles make the shark's skin feel like sandpaper.

Teeth
Sharks have sharp teeth and huge jaws. Great white sharks tear their food into mouth-sized pieces that they swallow whole.

Pectoral Fins
Pectoral fins on both sides of a shark's body control direction of movement.

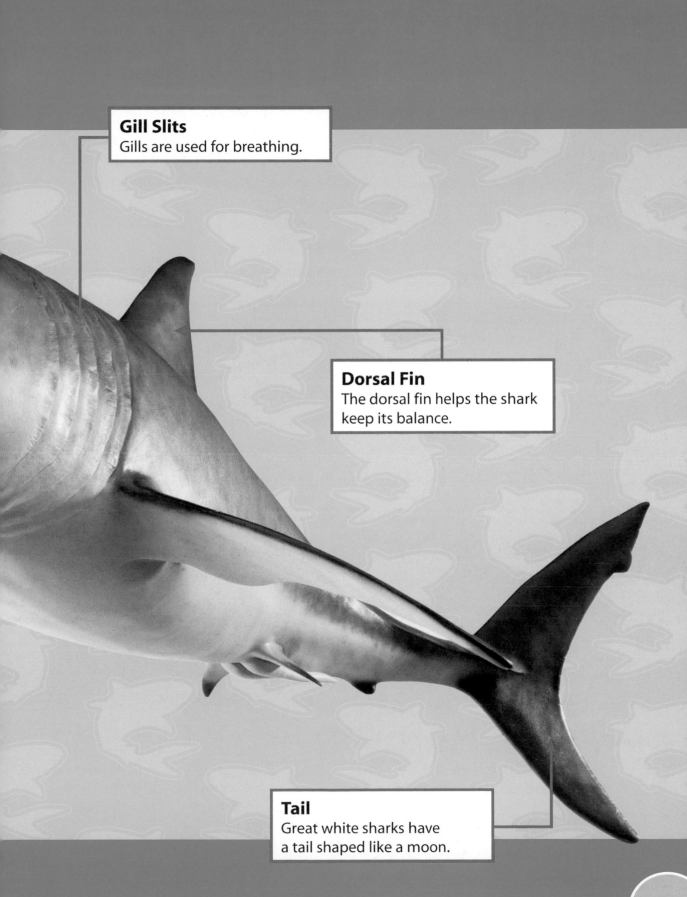

Gill Slits
Gills are used for breathing.

Dorsal Fin
The dorsal fin helps the shark keep its balance.

Tail
Great white sharks have a tail shaped like a moon.

How to Draw a Shark

1 Start by drawing a stick figure of the shark. Use circles for the head and body, and lines for the fins.

2 Now, join the two body circles together with smooth, curved lines starting from tip of the central line and ending before the tail fin.

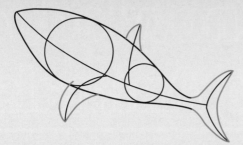

3 Now, draw the dorsal and tail fins and one of the pectoral fins.

4 In this step, draw the other pectoral fin, as shown.

5 Next, draw the eye, nostrils, and mouth.

6 Now, draw the teeth. Also, draw the small fins on the shark's underside.

7 Draw curved lines on the body, which will become the gill slits.

8 Erase the extra lines and the stick figure frame.

9 Color the picture.

Test Your Knowledge
of Amazing Animals

1. Alligators belong to what group of animals?

Answer: Reptiles

2. Are dolphins fish?

Answer: No. Dolphins are marine mammals.

3. What material are an elephant's tusks made of?

Answer: Ivory

4. What do gorillas mostly eat?

Answer: Plants

5. How large are lions' claws?

Answer: A lion's claws can be three inches (7.6 cm) long.

6. What is a shark's snout used for?

Answer: To smell

Want to learn more? Log on to av2books.com to access more content.

Draw an Environment

Materials
Large white poster board
Internet connection or library
Pencils and crayons or markers
Glue or tape

Steps

1. Complete one of the animal drawings in this book. Cut out the drawing.
2. Using this book, the internet, and a library, find out about your animal and the environment in which it lives.
3. Think about what the animal might see and hear in its environment. What does its environment look like? What sorts of trees are there? Is there water? What does the landscape look like? Are there other animals in its environment? What in the animal's environment is essential to its survival? What other important features might you find in the animal's environment?
4. On the large white poster board, draw an environment for your animal. Be sure to place all the features you noted in step 3.
5. Place the cutout animal in its environment with glue or tape. Color the animal's environment to complete the activity.

Glossary

communication: the sending and receiving of information

herbivores: animals that eat plants

imagination: the ability to form new creative ideas or images

mammals: animals that have fur, make milk, and are born live

marine mammals: warm-blooded animals that live in water

nostrils: openings on the nose that admit air and scents

opposable: the ability to place the first finger and the thumb together to grasp things

predators: animals that hunt other animals for food

prey: an animal that is hunted for food

snout: the projecting nose and mouth of an animal

Log on to www.av2books.com

AV² by Weigl brings you media enhanced books that support active learning. Go to www.av2books.com, and enter the special code found on page 2 of this book. You will gain access to enriched and enhanced content that supplements and complements this book. Content includes video, audio, web links, quizzes, a slide show, and activities.

Audio
Listen to sections of the book read aloud.

Video
Watch informative video clips.

Embedded Weblinks
Gain additional information for research.

Try This!
Complete activities and hands-on experiments.

WHAT'S ONLINE?

Try This!	Embedded Weblinks	Video	EXTRA FEATURES
Complete an interactive drawing tutorial for each of the six amazing animals in the book.	Learn more about each of the six amazing animals in the book.	Watch a video about amazing animals.	**Audio** Listen to sections of the book read aloud.
			Key Words Study vocabulary, and complete a matching word activity.
			Slide Show View images and captions, and prepare a presentation
			Quizzes Test your knowledge.

AV² was built to bridge the gap between print and digital. We encourage you to tell us what you like and what you want to see in the future.

Sign up to be an AV² Ambassador at www.av2books.com/ambassador.